Spring

Karen Bryant-Mole

RIGBY
INTERACTIVE
LIBRARY

Printed in China

05 04 03 02 01
10 9 8 7 6 5 4 3 2

Library of Congress Cataloging-in-Publication Data

Bryant-Mole, Karen.
   Spring / Karen Bryant-Mole.
    p. cm. — (Picture this!)   Includes index.
   Summary: Text and labeled photographs identify things associated with spring.
   ISBN 1-57572-055-8 (lib. bdg.)
    1. Spring—Juvenile literature. [1. Spring.] I. Title.
    II. Series: Bryant-Mole, Karen. Picture this!
QB637.5.B79   1997
508.2—dc21   97-396
                                 CIP
                                 AC

Text designed by Jean Wheeler

Acknowledgments

The publisher would like to thank the following for permission to reproduce photographs.
Cephas, p. 6.(left); Mick Rock, p. 17 (left); Helen Stylianou, p. 17 (right); M. Dutton/Eye Ubiquitous, p.4 (right); Keith Mullineaux, p. 20 (right); Frank Leather, p. 21 (left); Sue Passmore/Hutchison Library, p. 13 (left); Bernard Regent/Oxford Scientific Films, p.12 (left); Michael Leach, p. 13 (right); Martyn Chillmaid, p. 21 (right); Michael Richards/Tony Stone Images, p. 4 (left); Hans Reinhard, p. 5 (left); H. Richard Johnston, p. 5 (right), p. 8 (left); Niyati Reeve, p. 9 (right), Charlie Waite, p.9 (top); Gary Yeowell, p. 20 (left); Jeanne Drake/Zefa, p.9 (bottom); A&J Verkaik, p.12 (right).

Note to the Reader
Some words in this book may be new to you.
You may look them up in the glossary on page 24.

Contents

Flowers

In spring, the ground starts to warm up and flowers begin to bloom.

daffodils

bluebells

4

tulips

primrose

Spring Cleaning

Spring is the traditional time to clean you home from top to bottom.

dust pan and brush

sponge

rag

liquid
cleaner

window
cleaner

duster

7

Weather

Spring weather can bring sunshine and showers.

rain showers

sunshine

rainbow

tornado

Some places
have bad storms
in spring.

Clothes

These clothes are useful on a rainy spring day!

wind breaker

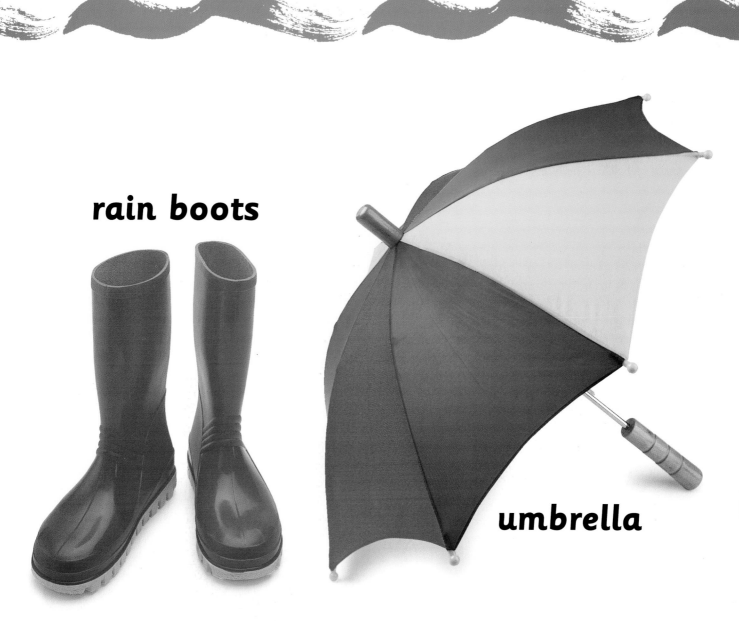

rain boots

umbrella

Trees

Many fruit trees grow flowers in spring.

plum

cherry

The flowers on fruit trees are sometimes called blossoms.

apple

pear

In the Garden

Spring is the time to plant
seeds in the garden.

trowel

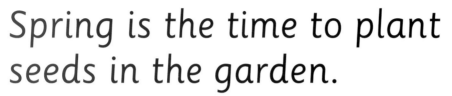

seeds

**garden
rake**

14

watering can

**seeds planted
in pots**

The flowers will bloom in summer.

Holidays

Many people celebrate these holidays in spring.

Passover

May Day

Easter

Holi

17

Vegetables

Here are some vegetables that can be bought in spring.

baby carrots

spring cabbage

new potatoes

spring onions

Baby Animals

Lots of baby animals are born in spring.

deer

ducks

sheep

swans

Do you know the names of these animals and their babies?

Nests

Many birds build their nests in spring.

Here are some things they might use.

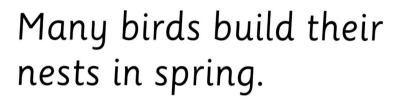

moss

feathers

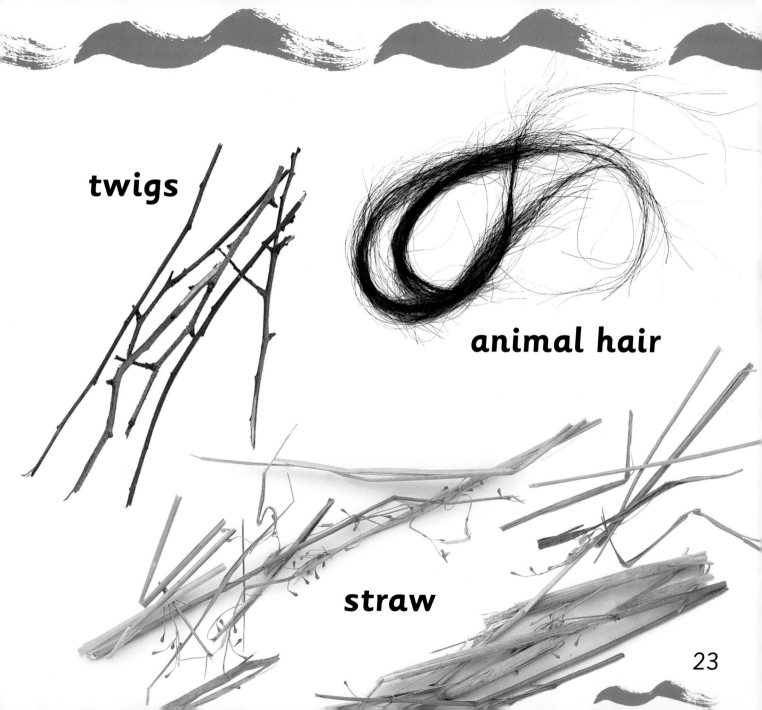

twigs

animal hair

straw

23

Glossary

bloom When flowers open out.
celebrate When people enjoy a holiday or other special occasion.
holi Hindu festival that celebrates the coming of spring.
tornado Very strong winds that whirl into a tube shape.
traditional Something that has happened for many years.

Index

Bryant-Mole, Karen
Spring (Picture this!)

DATE DUE

JUN 29 2013 MAR 29 2014		
APR 1 5 2014		
MAY 2 0 2014		
MAR 2 6 2016		
APR 2 5 2017		
MAR 1 4 2018		
MAR 1 4 2019		
MAY 2 5 2019		

DEMCO